POWERLESS

BUT NOT

HELPLESS

POWERLESS

BUT NOT

HELPLESS

Charles L. Allen

Fleming H. Revell Company
Tarrytown, New York

Scripture quotations are from the Holy Bible, New International Version. Copyright © 1973, 1978, 1984 International Bible Society. Used by permission of Zondervan Bible Publishers.

Appreciation is expressed to *The Atlanta Constitution* for permission to use part of the material in this book and to Alcoholics Anonymous for permission to quote the Twelve Steps.

This book was previously published under the title *12 Ways to Solve Your Problem*.

Library of Congress Cataloging-in-Publication Data

Allen, Charles Livingstone.
   Powerless but not helpless / Charles L. Allen.
     p.   cm.
   Rev. ed. of: 12 ways to solve your problem. 1961.
   ISBN 0-8007-5438-7
   1. Twelve-step programs—Religious aspects—Christianity. 2. Christian life—Methodist authors.
I. Allen, Charles Livingstone, 1913–   12 ways to solve your problem. II. Title.
BV4596.T88A45   1992
248.8′6—dc20   91-33313
                                    CIP

Copyright © 1954, 1961, 1992 by Charles L. Allen
Foreword Copyright © 1982 by
Foundation for Christian Living
Published by the Fleming H. Revell Company
Tarrytown, New York 10591
Printed in the United States of America

Contents

Foreword   9

THE STEPS SOLVE ANY PROBLEM   11

1. I ADMIT I NEED HELP   19
   *"We admitted we were powerless
   over alcohol—that our lives had
   become unmanageable."*

2. I BELIEVE GOD CAN HELP   25
   *"Came to believe that a Power
   greater than ourselves could restore
   us to sanity."*

3.   I DECIDE FOR GOD   31
     *"Made a decision to turn our will and
     our lives over to the care of God as
     we understood Him."*

4.   I LOOK AT MYSELF   37
     *"Made a searching and fearless moral
     inventory of ourselves."*

5.   I CONFESS MY WRONGS   43
     *"Admitted to God, to ourselves, and
     to another human being the exact
     nature of our wrongs."*

6.   I AM READY TO BE CHANGED   49
     *"Were entirely ready to have God
     remove all these defects of
     character."*

7. **I ASK GOD TO HELP** 55
   "Humbly asked Him to remove our shortcomings."

8. **I THINK OF THOSE I HAVE HARMED** 61
   "Made a list of all persons we had harmed, and became willing to make amends to them all."

9. **I MAKE AMENDS** 69
   "Made direct amends to such people wherever possible, except when to do so would injure them or others."

10. **I CONTINUE TO LOOK AT MYSELF** 75
    "Continued to take personal inventory and when we were wrong, promptly admitted it."

11.   I DRAW CLOSER TO GOD   83
      "Sought through prayer and
      meditation to improve our conscious
      contact with God as we understood
      Him, praying only for knowledge of
      His will for us and the power to
      carry that out."

12.   I HELP OTHERS   89
      "Having had a spiritual awakening as
      the result of these steps, we tried to
      carry this message to alcoholics and
      practice these principles in all our
      affairs."

Foreword

At a meeting of a small town Rotary Club I sat next to a friend who, years before, had won the victory over alcoholism.

"These last eight years, since I've been dry, have been wonderful years," said Jim. "Life was terrible before that."

"How did it all happen?" I asked. "Do you mind telling me again?"

"I can do all things through Christ who strengthens me," he quoted (Philippians 4:13).

"After I got in harmony with Him, I had all the strength I needed."

Over the years I have met a good many people who found wonder-working power the same way. Some, like Jim, had a drinking problem. Others had been plagued by all kinds of difficulties—family problems, discouragement, fear, feelings of inferiority, emotional disturbances, and so on. But all of them had found help in some of the principles of the Twelve Steps of Alcoholics Anonymous, the wonderful organization that helped Jim find the Higher Power.

In this book Dr. Charles L. Allen shows how well these Twelve Steps work in connection with any problem. It has done me good to read this book, and I believe it can help you, no matter what your problem may be. For as Dr. Allen says, "These Twelve Steps are really basic principles of the Christian faith."

NORMAN VINCENT PEALE

POWERLESS

BUT NOT

HELPLESS

THE
STEPS
SOLVE
ANY
PROBLEM

Once there was a man by the name of Bill who was a successful stockbroker in New York—successful until he became a drunk, hopeless in the eyes of most people and in his own sight. One morning he sat in the kitchen of his home drinking and talking to a non-drinking friend. His friend had found release from alcoholism through religious faith. But Bill could not go along with any "God concept." He would not admit that God could help him. That was in November.

In December he was in Towns Hospital being sobered up. His friend visited him again. After he left, "I realized," Bill says, "that I was powerless, hopeless, that I could not help myself and that nobody else could help me. In the midst of this I remembered this God business. I rose up in bed and said, 'If there be a God, let Him show Himself now.' All of a sudden, there was a light, a blinding white light that filled the whole room. A tremendous wind seemed to be blowing all around me and right through me. I felt that I stood in the presence of God. I felt an immense joy. And I was sure beyond all doubt that I was free from my obsession with alcohol."

Later Bill teamed up with Dr. Bob, who was also an alcoholic. Together they went to work to help other alcoholics and today there are thousands of people across the world who have found help, even complete victory, over alcoholism through the principles and encouragement of the organization they founded—Alcoholics Anonymous.

During my ministry I have worked with many people who had problems—not only alcoholism, but also various emotional disturbances, domestic difficulties, personality conflicts, job misfits, guilty consciences, fear, despair, loneliness, a sense of failure, and many other problems that destroy peace and purpose in life. As the pastor of churches in rural areas and in small towns; as a paid counselor in large industrial plants, in high schools, and on university campuses; and as pastor of a church on a main thoroughfare in a large city, I have had opportunities to minister to individuals.

While no two personal problems are the same, because no two people are the same, I have come to realize there are certain basic elements that are the same in nearly all these cases. I know that no person and no situation is hopeless. Sometimes one is humanly hopeless but the Bible says, "Put your hope in God" (Psalm 42:5). As long as one believes in God, there is hope. Again, the Bible says, "What is impossible with men is possible with God" (Luke 18:27).

I have learned it does not help to preach at people and call them sinners. Even though most of our problems come as a result of our own wrongdoing, we do not need condemnation. One's own conscience and the very problem itself is usually condemnation enough. When I go to my physician, though my illness may be my own fault, brought about because I disobeyed the laws of health, my physician's concern is making me well rather than shaming me for my past errors.

Also, I have learned that the basic solution to all personal problems is pretty much the same. Bill and Dr. Bob worked out a twelve-point Program of Recovery for the alcoholic. These same Twelve Steps work equally well, no matter what the trouble is. These are really basic principles of the Christian faith.

I
ADMIT
I
NEED
HELP

1

The first step of the Alcoholics Anonymous Program of Recovery is: *We admitted we were powerless over alcohol—that our lives had become unmanageable.* This is a step we frequently take with many problems of life. My car stops running and because I know that I do not know how to fix it, I call a mechanic. When I have a legal difficulty, I readily admit that I am not trained in the law and I go to a lawyer.

If I break my leg, I know that I cannot set it so I go to a physician. At times I need money I do not have, so I admit that I am financially powerless and go to a banker.

No person is completely self-sufficient. We depend on others to make most of our clothes, to provide most of our food, to make available to us most of the other necessities of life. I am writing these words on a dark night, yet my room is as light as the day. The darkness for me is conquered by the power company. Because I admit that I cannot conquer the darkness, I call upon the power company to do it for me.

Illustrations could be multiplied as to how we admit that we are powerless, that we cannot manage things by ourselves. But when it comes to the personal problems of our lives, our conceit gets in the way. Each of us likes to boast: "I am the master of my fate, I am the captain of my soul." As Lady Macbeth could not wash the stain from her guilty hands, neither can we handle many of our own weaknesses and situations.

Such an admission is hard to make. For example, take John, an alcoholic. He knows that liquor is a problem but he likes to boast he can stop whenever he really wants to. He sees others drinking who seem to be able to handle it and his false pride refuses to let him confess that he cannot do what someone else can. He remembers when he could take a drink or two and then leave it alone. But little by little a drink has become more important to him. He drinks alone. He learns the meaning of a hangover and the need for another drink to get started again. He gets to the point where one drink is too many but a hundred drinks are not enough.

In sober moments John realizes he needs to cut down, maybe even stop altogether. He makes himself believe he is still the boss over liquor, that he does not need help. And in that state of mind he is a slave, a chained prisoner; and since he cannot manage himself, until he knows that and admits it, he is hopeless and doomed.

Sometimes we have to suffer a great loss—business, friends, home, or self-respect—before we ever get honest with ourselves. In a dramatic scene, Nathan the prophet shook his finger in the face of King David and cried, "You are the man!" (2 Samuel 12:7). David had done wrong. He became convicted of his wrong. He also recognized that he was powerless over his wrong and thus he came to God to plead His forgiving mercy and help (Psalm 51).

"I admit that I cannot handle this matter alone" is not a confession of weakness. It is the mark of a courageous and sensible person.

I
BELIEVE
GOD
CAN
HELP

2

After admitting we lack the power within ourselves, the second step in the Program of Recovery, which may be applied to any personal
problem, is *to believe that a Power greater
than ourselves can restore us to sanity.* That
"Power greater than ourselves" is God. I have
in my study a book of some 600 pages which
gives all the arguments for the existence of
God. When I started to preach I used that

book a great deal, but now I have no use for it. I have learned you cannot find God through argument.

When someone tells me she doesn't believe in God, I like to quote a scene from Lloyd Douglas's *Invitation to Live*. Sally had failed as an actress. She had thrown away her great opportunity because of her conceit, disregard of authority, and blindness to her own limitations. Defeated, discouraged, and cynical, she said to the dean, "I'm not even sure that I believe in God."

"That's not important just now," he replied. "I mean, it isn't quite so urgent, at present, whether you believe in God as whether He can believe in you. If you will conduct yourself in a manner that might encourage Him to believe in you, the time may come when you can feel that you should return the compliment."

Four of the Ten Commandments deal with our relationship to God and the proper attitude toward Him. Nowhere in the Bible, however, are we commanded to believe in God on a purely intellectual basis. The fact is we instinctively believe just as we instinctively hunger and thirst. You do not need to teach a baby to hunger. But our instinct to believe and to worship can be perverted. Though we cannot stop the flow of a river, we can change its course. Humans are made so that they are compelled to worship something, but they can worship the wrong things.

Not in every case, but in many cases, I have found that people with emotional problems have abnormally inflated egos. Many are like a character described by a modern novelist: "Edith was a little country bounded on the north, south, east, and west by Edith."

It is so easy to become self-centered and then to become sensitive. Being sensitive we become easily hurt and our personal problems multiply. We notice every little slight by other people, we become jealous, our pride leads to unkind feelings toward others. We are hard to get along with. We live within our own little world with ourselves as our god, and thus we become out of harmony with the rest of the world. Everything goes wrong.

However, having finally despaired of our ability to be our own god, to save ourselves, we look to a Power greater than ourselves and immediately we become possessed by a new hope. One of the greatest pieces of literature on earth is Tennyson's *In Memoriam*. In that classic we find this expression: "The mighty hopes that make us men."

Believing in God, one begins to realize that there is no hopeless person and no hopeless situation. Immediately, despair, melancholy, and useless remorse are swept away and under the power of a "mighty hope," one begins to be a real person again.

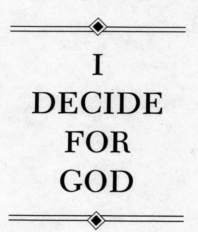

I
DECIDE
FOR
GOD

3

We made a decision to turn our will and our lives over to the care of God as we understood Him is the third step of recovery for any person. The first step is to admit that we cannot save ourselves and the second step is to believe in God, who can save us. Now, third, we put our lives into harmony with God's will.

The phrase I especially want to underscore is, "God as we understand Him." The picture of God in our minds determines our attitude toward Him. Fortunately, we have a perfect picture of God given us by the One who knew God best. Jesus told this story:

There was a boy who found home and the rule of his father bothersome. He wanted to cast aside his father's restraints, to take over complete management of his own life.

So he went out on his own, living by his inclinations and his animal appetite. Eventually he found himself in a pen with animals like himself, hogs. Not every rebel against God's higher will goes to what we call the "gutter." Some people gain all their earthly desires and have all the things their bodies want. But humans are more than physical bodies. Each person has a soul and the soul has desires, too.

Down in the hog pen—the place of mere physical satisfaction—the boy "came to himself." That is one of the most astute phrases in the Bible. Man is not a single self. There is a greedy self, a passionate self, a careless self, and other selves. But also, in every person there is that self that Shakespeare had in mind when he wrote: "To thine own self be true." It is our best self. I have had people tell me, "I am not myself." That is an exact statement. It is a high moment in any life when one "comes to himself."

As a result, the boy says, "I have sinned." He is honest with himself and admits that he has been wrong. He realizes he is powerless to save himself. He knows there is one who can save him. So he makes the decision to come back to the father, to accept his will and way of life. All that is preliminary to the picture of God Jesus wants us to have. Let me quote Christ's exact words:

"So he got up and went to his father. But while he was still a long way off, his father saw him and was filled with compassion for him; he ran to his son, threw his arms around him and kissed him. . . . The father said to his servants, 'Quick! Bring the best robe and put it on him. Put a ring on his finger and sandals on his feet. Bring the fattened calf and kill it. Let's have a feast and celebrate. For this son of mine was dead and is alive again; he was lost and is found' " (Luke 15:20–24).

There is God! Not one word of condemnation. No reminding the boy of past mistakes. No effort to humiliate him. Instead, he is welcomed back home and is restored. It is not difficult to turn our will and our lives over to God when we understand He is like that.

Any time we desire, we can assume the management of our own lives. God is not a jailer, He is a father. We talk about the "House of God," not the penitentiary. We are free to leave Him out of our lives. But let us be thankful, we are free any time to come back to Him and be assured of welcome. The decision must be ours.

I
LOOK
AT
MYSELF

4

In the solution of any problem, an important step is *to make a searching and fearless moral inventory of ourselves*. Usually the main trouble is not some outward condition; it is within ourselves. As Thomas Carlyle said, "Always there is a black spot in our sunshine—the shadow of ourselves." One of the greatest preachers and men of all time was Dwight L. Moody. He said, "I've had more trouble with

D. L. Moody than with any man I know."
When we get ourselves right, then our world
gets right. But if we are wrong inside, then
everything else for us goes wrong.

In my work with alcoholics, for example, I
have found a number of causes, and rarely is
liquor the primary problem. It may date back
to childhood when one was abusively treated,
or was made to feel inferior, or grew up without a sense of security. A guilty conscience can
wreak havoc with a person. Judas reached the
point where he could not stand to live with
himself so he went out and hanged himself.
Some get drunk, some go into emotional hys-
teria, some become hypercritical, and so on.

Disappointment, thwarted ambition, lack of
self-confidence, and dissatisfaction with life as
we are forced to live it are some of the basic
causes of personal problems. Other causes may
be loneliness, physical pain, or a great sorrow.
A broken heart can take the fight out of a person
and destroy the will to live. When Sir Harry

Lauder heard the news that his son had been killed, he said: "In a time like this there are three courses open to one: (1) He may give way to despair, sour on the world, and become a grouch. (2) He may endeavor to drown his sorrows in drink or by a life of waywardness and wickedness. (3) Or he may turn to God."

A young lady who came to see me was bitterly against getting married. Though she had opportunities to marry, she would not give up her freedom for any man, she said. She was very unhappy. In analyzing her feelings we discovered that marriage was really what she wanted most of all. But she had crossed the moral lines and felt in her heart unfit for marriage. Instead of hating marriage, actually she was hating herself. When we settled the sin-consciousness of her heart through a genuine experience of repentance and the forgiveness of God and herself, her attitude was completely changed, her very personality was made new.

A mother who came to see me was neurotic. Tracing back, we came to the time her only son was killed. We talked about death and its meaning; about eternal life and the "Father's House"; about releasing our loved ones to God. As her faith in God increased, and with it her confidence in God's eternal purposes, she settled the question of the loss of one she loved very much. Her own personality difficulties were then settled also.

I have suggested to many that they start back as far as memory goes and write down the unsettled wrongs in their lives. Then I have suggested that they ask honestly, "What can I now do about each thing I have listed?" If we do what is right and reasonable, and as we settle those things that have been in our way, it is amazing how quickly our problems vanish. It takes time, effort, and most of all courage to make "a searching and fearless moral inventory," but it must be done.

I
CONFESS
MY
WRONGS

5

Nothing helps like honest confession and, without confession, usually nothing else can help. A lady came to Sigmund Freud suffering from what seemed to be an incurable disease. She wanted to tell him her troubles but he insisted he could not help her. However, because she would not take no for an answer, he let her come regularly each week. She told her story at great length. After a time he discovered she was actually getting well. That was really the beginning of the practice of psychiatry as we know it. In my own ministry I have seen miracles accomplished just by telling the story.

As you read Psalm 23, you know the writer was a man of poise and power. Within his soul there were no conflicts. His own problems were solved. But it was not always so with him. David had done wrong. Instead of getting mad at Nathan, his preacher, for pointing out his wrong, David went to his knees in confession. Fortunately, we have the confession that saved him. It will save us, too. It is Psalm 51. Notice the confession steps he takes.

1. "Have mercy on me, O God." Justice is not enough. Only when we believe in and accept the loving mercy of God does forgiveness become possible.

2. "I know my transgressions." He does not talk about how others have done as badly as or worse than he. He pleads no mitigating cir-

cumstances. He does not excuse himself. He has done wrong and is man enough to say so.

3. "Wash me, and I will be whiter than snow." He has faith that forgiveness can be his. No matter what he has done, because he believes in God he has hope. There is no sin God cannot cancel.

4. "Create in me a pure heart." He wants to be guilty no more. His repentance is genuine because he is willing to change. One definition of repentance is to change one's mind in regard to one's conduct.

5. "Restore to me the joy of your salvation." He recognizes that happiness can come to one only as a result of a right relationship with God.

6. "Then I will teach transgressors your ways." If he is healed, he will not be ashamed of the physician. He will put his life into useful service.

The fifth step in the Program of Recovery is:

We admitted to God, to ourselves, and to another human being the exact nature of our wrongs. It is the step of confession, sometimes hard to take but necessary.

This does not mean we should go shouting all our faults to every person we meet. While honest confession is good for the soul, it can be bad for the reputation. "To God, to ourselves, and to another human being," the confession should be made. The other human being must be a trusted friend, and usually it should be one professionally trained to hear our confession—a minister or physician, for example. And, even though our wrongs may have been in connection with some other person, let's confine our confession to ourselves. Let the other person do his own confessing.

We are promised: "If we confess our sins, he is faithful and just and will forgive us our sins and purify us from all unrighteousness" (1 John 1:9).

I
AM
READY
TO
BE
CHANGED

6

After confession, to overcome our problems we must take the sixth step of the Program of Recovery, which is: *We were entirely ready to have God remove all these defects of character.* One of the greatest saints of all time was Augustine. But there was a shameful chapter of wrong living in his life. He knew he was wrong, that he should be changed. So he would pray, "Lord, make me pure," and then his nerve would fail, so he would add, "but not now." Most of us know what our mistakes are, we know what we ought to do about them, and someday we intend to do what we should, but so often we are defeated by the simple device of waiting until tomorrow.

There is an old story of Satan seeking a plan to destroy the world. He called in his chief assistants. First came Anger, who said, "Let me go and destroy men and women. I will so antagonize them with one another that they will destroy themselves." Next came Lust, saying, "I will defile their minds that they will become beasts."

Greed said, "Allow me to go and I can so eliminate all control they have over their desires that they will destroy themselves." Gluttony, Envy, Jealousy, and Hate each told of their plans. Idleness claimed he could do the job of destroying humankind.

But with none of these was Satan satisfied.

Finally, his last assistant came in. This one said, "I shall talk to humans persuasively in terms of all that God wants them to be. I shall tell them how fine their plans and resolutions are to be honest, clean, and brave. I shall encourage them in the good purpose of life."

Satan was aghast at such talk. But the assistant continued, "However, I shall persuade them there is no hurry, that they can do all those things sometime later. I shall advise them to wait until conditions become more favorable before they start." Satan became enthusiastic. He cried, "You are the one I shall send to earth to destroy humankind." It was Procrastination—just put it off a while longer.

To me the most disappointing play in baseball is to see a batter let the third strike be called on him. He might fly out, hit a foul, ground out, hit into a double play, or he might get a hit, if he swings at the ball. But just to stand there with his bat on his shoulder and go out by doing nothing is to me the worst possible course. Yet I know a lot of people who go through life with their bats on their shoulders. They are going to do something, but they never get ready.

Once someone was seeking the answer to "What do you think of Christ?" Youth replied, "I am too young to think." Adulthood said, "I am too busy now to think." Maturity said, "I am too anxious to think." Old age replied, "My habits are so fixed I cannot now think." Death said, "It is too late to think." Eternity replied, "I have forever to think." But in eternity it is too late.

Someone wrote these lines: "He was going to be all a mortal should be, tomorrow. . . . And all that he left when living was through, Was a mountain of things he intended to do."

Until you say, "I am ready," not even God can help you.

I
ASK
GOD
TO
HELP

7

If we have a tooth that needs to be pulled, we go to a dentist. If we have an appendix that needs to come out, we let a surgeon do the job. If a watch is not keeping correct time, we take it to a jeweler. If there is a knock in the motor of our car, we take it to a mechanic. But when we ourselves are out of adjustment, when there are defects in character, and when weakness of mind and soul is destroying much of the peace and joy of life, we decide we can make the necessary corrections ourselves. We decide we will do better, we turn over a "new leaf," we think we are sufficient unto ourselves. By tinkering with ourselves, we think we are able to save ourselves.

So we read a "self-help" book, we set out to keep busy or take a vacation, to forgive ourselves and forget the past, to make changes in our thinking. But any program of self-salvation ultimately fails. Just as a man cannot lift himself by pulling up on his own bootstraps, neither does a man have within himself the power to save himself. Thus the seventh step in the Program of Recovery is: *Humbly ask God to remove our shortcomings.*

God is both able and willing and whenever we decide we need God and ask His help, He will work miracles within our lives. As Saint Paul expressed it: "My power is made perfect in weakness" (2 Corinthians 12:9). That is, realizing my weakness, it becomes possible for the strength of God to come into my life. Sometimes it takes a severe setback to make us realize our weakness and put us on our knees.

A mother from a small town came to see me. A year before, her daughter had come to the big city and during the year had "outgrown" her mother. The mother's letters were unanswered, and on holiday and weekend trips the daughter had some other place to go instead of visiting home. Finally, the mother had come to the city to visit the daughter, though she was not invited. The daughter was ashamed of the mother's clothes and manners. She was very rude. Brokenhearted, the mother came to see me. I told her a story:

Once a shepherd had a wayward sheep. The sheep would not recognize the shepherd's voice, would not accept the shepherd's care and guidance. One day the sheep slipped and broke its leg. Now it could not walk. Gently the shepherd carried it and ministered to it. When the leg was healed, the sheep had come to love the shepherd.

I suggested to the mother that she wait patiently, but while she waits that she pray, and keep the love in her heart and be ready. Maybe one day the daughter will not be sufficient unto herself. She may become lonely or frightened or ill. While she is strong she has no need of the one who loves her the most, but one day she may become weary. Her heart, so full of life and laughter, may someday be broken. Then she will need that mother and of her own will, she will come home.

So God is waiting. He does not push Himself upon us. But when we are driven to our knees by our own insufficiency, God is there to lift us up and save us. God does not do for us what we think we can do for ourselves.

I

THINK

OF

THOSE

I

HAVE

HARMED

8

Many stories have been told about the painting of Leonardo da Vinci's *The Last Supper*. One of the best is that da Vinci made the face of Judas similar in appearance to a personal enemy. As the artist thought of how much he disliked this man, it was easy to put a face on the canvas to represent Judas, one who would sell out his Lord. However, when he came to paint the face of Jesus, he had

great difficulty. His eyes would wander to
the face of his enemy and the thoughts en-
gendered within his own mind made it impossible to concentrate on the beauty and
purity of Christ. He succeeded in painting
the face of Christ only after he painted out
the face of Judas and reconciled himself with
his enemy.

No person can become good and strong
with a wrong spirit in his or her heart toward
any person. So the eighth step in the Alcoholics Anonymous Program of Recovery,
steps that will bring about the recovery of
any person no matter what the trouble, is:
*Made a list of all persons we had harmed,
and became willing to make amends to them
all.* That is the teaching of Christ, who said:
"If you are offering your gift at the altar and
there remember that your brother has something against you, leave your gift there in
front of the altar. First go and be reconciled

to your brother; then come and offer your gift" (Matthew 5:23, 24).

In making a list of the persons we have harmed, let's start first with our own family circle. It is strange but true that we will be the unkindest to the ones we love the most. Love is not the only virtue that begins at home. Brotherhood and human love, if it is to begin at all, must begin at home. In describing a true home, someone said: "Home, a world of strife shut out, a world of love shut in. . . . The place where our stomachs get three meals a day and our hearts a thousand. . . . Where the faults and failings of each other are hidden under a blanket of love. . . . Where the great are small and the small are great. . . . The father's kingdom, the mother's world, the child's paradise."

When we married we promised to "love, honor, and keep" the one we chose. We promised "to have and to hold . . . for better or worse, for richer for poorer, in sickness and in health, to love and to cherish. . . ." Have I really done that? Have I been the father or the mother my children had a right to expect? If any person's life is not what he wants it to be, the place to start making it right is at home. If at the close of a day one can walk up the steps to a happy home, one finds power and peace.

In listing those we have wronged, next let us think of our friends. No person has many close friends and thus we cannot afford to lose even one. Elizabeth Barrett Browning once said to Charles Kingsley, "What is the secret of your life? Tell me that I may make mine beautiful, too." Kingsley's simple reply was, "I have a friend."

After our families and our friends, let us list any others we may have wronged. We may think of someone who has wronged us, but that is no excuse for our returning evil for evil. Think of our attitude toward people we merely meet in passing, the stranger on the street. A father once said to his son, "Remember that you show courtesy to others, not because they are gentlemen, but because you are."

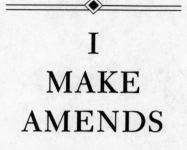

I
MAKE
AMENDS

9

Once there was a man by the name of Zac-
chaeus, whose one purpose in life was getting
ahead and taking care of himself. He took ad-
vantage of every person he could; he was
grasping, greedy, and selfish. One day, however, he got a close look at Christ. Then the
supreme purpose of his life was changed. Instead of what he could get, he became concerned with what he could be. Being a real

man became important to him. But standing in his way were the wrongs he had done other people. So he said, "If I have cheated anybody out of anything, I will pay back four times the amount" (Luke 19:8). No person can be what he or she ought without restitution. So the ninth step of the Program of Recovery for any person is: *Make direct amends to people we have harmed whenever possible, except when to do so would injure them or others.*

We can't just forget it when we are able to do something about it. A letter came to me the other day from a man in another city. He enclosed a check for $50 and told me that at one time he had worked in a drugstore. He had taken some money wrongfully. The man who owned the store had died but he understood the druggist's daughter was now a nurse in my city. He asked if I would please locate her and give her the check. I was happy to do it. It was not easy for that man to send the check, but in the sending of it he experienced a great joy and release worth far more than the money involved. Without the sending of the check, his recovery would have been impossible.

If we have harmed any person in any way, and if there is anything we can now do about it, we must do it. It may be an apology, or some service we can render. On the other hand, there are some wrongs about which nothing can be done. In that case we can eliminate all wrong feeling we hold toward that person. We can begin loving that person and praying for him or her. Sometimes that is harder to do than returning stolen money.

The greatest harm we can do to any person is the withholding of love. When I hold wrong feelings toward another, my very thoughts go out to that person and rob that person of inner peace. Likewise, my thoughts of love are felt by the one I love and give to her strength and joy. Our brains are actually broadcasting our thoughts. I do not have to commit a wrong act toward another, I do not even have to see the other person; I can definitely harm him or her just by my thoughts.

I prescribed the thirteenth chapter of 1 Corinthians to a lady recently. That is the chapter which tells us what love is and what it does. Love is patient, is kind, does not envy, is not conceited, is unselfish, is not easily angered, does not think evil, trusts, hopes, and endures. I told her to read that chapter thoughtfully and prayerfully every day for a month, thinking of the person she felt unkindly toward as she read. I have seen that prescription work miracles, not only in the one thinking the thoughts, but also in the one who was the object of the thoughts.

Restitution is never easy but in some form it is always essential, if we really want to be healthy both in body and in soul.

I
CONTINUE
TO
LOOK
AT
MYSELF

10

There is a verse in the Bible that warns: "If you think you are standing firm, be careful that you don't fall!" (1 Corinthians 10:12). In baseball there is an expression: "The game is never over until the last man is out." In the building of a life, the complete victory is never won until the life is over. So the tenth step in the Program of Recovery is: *Continued to take personal inventory and when we were wrong promptly admitted it.* In *Pilgrim's Progress*, John Bunyan puts a pathway leading to hell even at the gate of heaven. He is teaching the lesson that though we climb to the very gate, there is still the danger of being lost. We strive for perfection but along the way we must daily meet the struggle.

The way to win in life is to fix within our minds the goal and keep moving toward it. As Tennyson expressed it: "And oh, for a man to rise in me, That the man I am may cease to be." There is a legend of a prince who had a crooked back. One day he said to his most skillful sculptor: "Make a statue of me, but with a straight back. I would see myself as I might have been."

When the statue was finished the prince put it in a secret place where only he could see it. Every day the prince would slip away to look longingly and earnestly at the statue. Months passed and people began to notice the prince's back was not as crooked as it used to be. He continued to look at the perfect statue and each time the sight of it set his blood tingling and his heart throbbing, until one day he realized that his back was straight. He had become the man of the statue.

We all have faults and daily we must recognize those faults, but we overcome them by the power of a vision of ourselves as we would like to be. And if the vision is clear enough, the struggle to attain it is never too hard. One of the greatest writers of all time was Robert Louis Stevenson. He once wrote to a friend: "For fourteen years I have not had one day of real health. I have wakened sick and gone to bed weary, and yet I have done my work unflinchingly. I have written my books in bed and out of bed, written them when I was worn by coughing, written them during hemorrhages, written them when my head swam from weakness. But the battle goes on—ill or well is a trifle so long as it goes."

Recently, in a hospital for alcoholics, I met a man who told me a story all too familiar. For seven years he had remained sober. Not one drink had he taken during this time. Then one night he was walking home with a friend from work. The friend suggested they stop for a beer. He only intended to get a soft drink but when he saw the beer he decided that just one would not hurt him. After all, he had gone seven years now and was safe, he reasoned. He drank that beer and now for four years he has been struggling to get back on the drinkless trail again, but as yet he hasn't been able to make it.

It is so easy to be thrown off guard. Rarely does one deliberately plan to fail, but something happens. Our feelings get hurt, a great sorrow may come, we may have a streak of bad luck, we are lonely or sorry for ourselves, or some crisis develops. And in a moment's time all the fine victories we have worked so hard to win can be swept away. So we must watch our weakness and keep our eyes firmly fixed on a high goal.

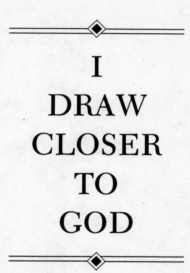

I
DRAW
CLOSER
TO
GOD

11

The eleventh step in the Alcoholics Anonymous Program of Recovery, steps that will
solve any problem of one's life, is: *Sought
through prayer and meditation to improve our
conscious contact with God as we understood
Him, praying only for knowledge of His will
for us and the power to carry that out.* With a
God such as we have, a person is foolish to try
to live without His guidance and power.

In my own church every Sunday night we sing a little chorus: "Only believe, only believe, all things are possible, only believe." I know that if people will believe they can conquer. It was Jesus who said, "Everything is possible for him who believes" (Mark 9:23). Again, He said, "What is impossible with men is possible with God" (Luke 18:27).

We defeat ourselves with our very thoughts. Listen to people talk and you will see what I mean. Better still, listen to yourself. We get up in the morning and say, "I guess it will rain. This is going to be a bad day." . . . "I know I won't get a seat on the bus into town and I hate to stand up." . . . "I don't feel well. I think I am getting a cold." . . . "I don't suppose I will sleep well tonight" . . . and so we talk ourselves into one defeat after another. Dr. Paul du Bois, the great Swiss psychotherapist, laid great emphasis on the power of words. He advised people to learn words like *victorious, invulnerable, imperturbable,* and to say them until they became a part of them.

But just our words are not enough. Daniel A. Poling says that when he first awakens in the morning he says, "I believe, I believe." He says it over and over until he actually does believe. Then he thinks of some things he believes—that he will have opportunities today, that he will be able to meet whatever crisis may arise, that this will be a good day for him. Most of all, he believes in God. When we believe in God, defeat words are eliminated from our vocabulary.

Though we recognize our own weaknesses, we also recognize God's power. So we begin to put ourselves into God's hands. We become anxious to put out of our lives and minds anything that prevents His Spirit from flowing into us. So we cease thinking of how we can control ourselves; we become concerned with how God can control us. Gladly we surrender ourselves to God. And as we become God-centered and God-controlled, our lives become victorious.

Whenever we really want to know God's will for our lives, we will find it. E. Stanley Jones lists eight ways to find God:

1. Through the life and teachings of Jesus as contained in the Scriptures.

2. Through the accumulated wisdom of the centuries, mediated to us through the church.

3. Through disciplined group guidance.

4. Through individual counsel.

5. Through opening providences.

6. Through the discovery of natural law by scientific investigation.

7. Through our heightened moral intelligence.

8. Through the inner voice.

Each day in our lives we should be more conscious of God than we were the day before.

I
HELP
OTHERS

12

Some time ago I was visiting an elderly woman who has suffered almost unbearable pain through many years. Yet I found her to be one of the most radiant, happy people I have known. During our conversation she told me of her son who has missed the way and almost wrecked his life. In the early days of her intense suffering, she asked God why He was keeping her on earth. She understood God's answer to be: "I am keeping you here so that you might pray for that boy." Through the years she has been faithful to that task. I wish I could say that her prayers had been successful in saving her boy, but it seems that as yet such is not the case. But, and this is important, praying for someone else has brought victory and beauty into her own life.

The Twelve Step recovery program begins with a recognition of our own inability to save ourselves and leads us to faith in God and a right relationship with other people. The final step is: *Having had a spiritual awakening as the result of these steps, we tried to carry this message to alcoholics and practice these principles in all our affairs.* That simply means, having been saved ourselves, we seek to save others.

Dwight L. Moody said, "I speak to some person every day about his soul. Even if it does not help him, it keeps me warm." As our

Lord put it: "Whoever loses his life for my sake will find it" (Matthew 10:39).

Once a man jumped into the river to drown himself. A friend saw him jump and immediately jumped in to save him. It so happened that the man who wanted to drown himself was an expert swimmer, but the man who was trying to save him could not swim at all. Though the first man wanted to die, he did not want to see his friend drown. So he set out to save the man who had jumped in to help him. In saving his friend, life took on new meaning for him—so much so that he decided he wanted to live.

There is an old Oriental story of a man who was in hell. He pleaded with the gods for release. They asked him what good he had done in life. All he could remember was that one day, while walking in the woods, he saw a spider and did not kill it. At once the thin, silvery thread of a spider web was let down to him. He seized the thread and was slowly being lifted out of hell. His fellow sufferers, seeing him about to escape, clutched his garment and his feet, and all were lifted up together. The man, fearing the web might break, cried, "Let go! Let go!" But when they let go, the thread broke. In short, the thread was strong enough to lift all together, but it could not bear the heavy burden of a selfish soul.

In the early days of the Christian Church when believers were suffering almost unbearable persecution, they drew so closely together that a historian of that time was inspired to write, "How they love one another." It was the strength each gained in seeking to encourage the others that firmly implanted the church and made it triumphant over the enemy. We simply cannot build a great life alone. We save ourselves by saving others.